THE POPULARITY GAME

HOW TO BE POPULAR IN SOCIAL GROUPS

VERONICA HEART

CONTENTS

SOCIAL RANKS

To be popular is one of the strongest desires of people in every society. To be liked, noticed, adored, admired, respected, worshiped, are some of the things that come with popularity. Who wouldn't want to be popular? The opposite of side of popularity consists of being rejected, criticized, hated, and lonely.

In simple terms, the more people that know you, like and support you, the more popular you are judged to be. It means being accepted socially. The more positive attention you get, the more popular you will become. To get positive attention you must have five qualities: physical beauty, fashion sense, personality, social skills, and status symbols.

There are two main types of popularity, sociometric popularity, and perceived popularity. Sociometric popularity, common in adulthood, is typically a result of being well-liked. Perceived popularity, the more common type in high school social hierarchy, is a result of visible reputation and social status.

In some social circles or stages of life, there is a stricter social hierarchy. For example, high school popularity has a stricter social hierarchy than adulthood. There are different levels of popularity and there are advantages and disadvantages to each level.

This book focuses mainly on high school popularity. Be warned: This book is superficial in many ways but society at large can be very superficial. Sometimes we need to be superficial to get what we want, regardless of who we truly are as a person.

Unlike some books, which base their information on the opinions and experiences of the author, this book is based on research studies and public opinion surveys.

MALE SOCIAL HIERARCHY

Alpha Male

The Alpha Male, the dominant leader among men, is at the highest level of popularity. He tends to be the strongest and most intimidating. He has strong confidence and attitude. He tends to be handsome and the most masculine among a group of men. All the women are attracted to him, while all the men want to be him, or at least be his friend. In adulthood, the Alpha Male is successful and wealthy with a very beautiful wife.

Beta Male

Beta Males are the sidekicks of the Alpha Male and are up for anything the Alpha wants to do. Betas are not as socially dominant as the Alpha but are nevertheless confident and attractive to women.

Gamma Male

The Gamma Male doesn't seek approval or abide by social hierarchy. He does his own thing and creates his own rules. Gammas lack assertiveness, freely demonstrate their emotions, and aren't very interested in status symbols and attaining popularity.

Delta Male

Deltas are the great majority of men. Deltas tend to put females on pedestals. They greatly admire the Alpha Male and his ability to attract women.

Omega Male

Omega Males are ranked on the lowest level of social hierarchy. They are not confident, strong, or attractive to women. They are typically mistreated by the Alpha Male and the Beta Male. They are rejected in social settings.

FEMALE SOCIAL HIERARCHY

Queen Bee

Queen Bees, who are the leaders of a woman's clique, are at the highest level of popularity. They are the ones with the most highly developed personality, social skills, fashion sense, and beauty. They tend to be the prettiest and most feminine among a group of women.

Beta Female

After the Queen Bee the next most popular is the Beta Female. She is the Queen Bee's closest friend. She also has a highly developed personality, social skills, fashion sense, and beauty but to a lesser degree. There are occasionally more than one Beta Female.

Gamma Female

The Gamma Female doesn't seek approval or abide by social hierarchy. She does her own thing and creates her own rules. Gammas aren't very interested in status symbols and attaining popularity.

Delta Female

Deltas are the great majority of females. They try to fit in as best they can. Deltas tend to put the Alpha Male and Alpha Female on a pedestal. They greatly admire the Queen Bee and her ability to attract men.

Omega Female

Omega Females are ranked on the lowest level of social hierarchy. They are not pretty and can't attract men. They lack social skills. They are typically mistreated by the Queen Bee and the Beta Female. They are rejected in social settings.

CHAPTER ONE

PHYSICAL BEAUTY

Physical beauty is one of the most important factors in the popularity game since it's always the first things people notice and it is highly valued in society. Therefore, men and women with physical attractiveness have a head start in the popularity game. The prettiest women and the most handsome men are the strongest players.

A study found that physically attractive people are more popular than less attractive people and people are more likely to have an interaction with people who are physically attractive (Source: A. Feingold. (1992). Good-looking people are not what we think. *Psychological Bulletin*, 11, 304-341).

Ugly people are rejected socially. In one study, people avoided sitting next to people with physical deformities (Source: Houston, R. Bull. (1994). Do people avoid sitting next to someone who is facially disfigured? *European Journal of Social Psychology*, 24, 279-284).

Physically attractive individuals are regarded more positively in first impressions. The physical attractiveness stereotype is a term that psychologists use to refer to the tendency to assume that people who are physically attractive also possess other socially desirable personality traits.

A famous quote states that "Beauty is in the eye of the beholder," meaning that the perception of beauty is subjective. However, scientists have discovered that this is simply not true. Studies have shown that people in every culture are using the same criteria in their judgments of physical attractiveness. There is an acceptable and unacceptable way of looking.

Scientists that analyze beauty have found that there are physical features that are found in every attractive human being. The most attractive people have large eyes, a small nose, immaculate skin, impeccable hair, and fit bodies.

LARGE EYES

The very first thing most people notice is the eyes. Large, almond-shaped eyes are considered the most attractive. There are various methods of creating the illusion of larger eyes.

For men, start by getting your eyebrows cleaned up at an eyebrow threading salon. By getting your eyebrows cleaned up you can make your eyes appear bigger.

The next step is to use a colorless mascara. Colorless mascara will make your eyelashes longer, which makes the eyes look bigger. Do not use black mascara, unless you want to look like a girl and be ridiculed.

To grow your lashes use Latisse, a prescription solution that produces longer, thicker eyelashes. Careprost and Lumigan are the generic versions of Latisse and are available from www.alldaychemist.com and www.worldwide-pharmacies.com.

For women, the easiest method of causing the eyes to appear larger is with the use of makeup. Ideally, you should go to a makeup artist to request a lesson in making the eyes appear bigger with makeup. If you are good with makeup, you can try experimenting with makeup and do it yourself. For the best makeup results, use makeup by MAC Cosmetics, NARS Cosmetics, or makeup purchased at Sephora.

All makeup artists will tell you that white eye shadow and white eyeliner gives the illusion of larger eyes when properly applied. White eye shadow and white eyeliner should be a small-eyed girl's best friend.

Start by applying a cream or off-white eyeshadow on your eyelids. Then, use a medium brown eye shadow and shade in a high crease right below your brow bone and draw it out beyond the end of your eyes.

Line your waterline with a cream or off-white eyeliner. Do not use pure, bright white since it will look too obvious.

Even though the use of black eyeliner around the eyes is common, do not draw black liner in your waterline. It will make your eyes look smaller. Instead, use a medium brown eye shadow and precisely line under the waterline.

Finally, the most important step is to apply false eyelashes or apply a black mascara with a false eyelash effect. False eyelashes that are at least half an inch long make the eyes look larger. The smaller your eyes are, the longer the false eyelashes you should use. Get a professional makeup artist to teach you how to apply false eyelashes and get the makeup artist to apply the false eyelashes on you for the first few times.

Eyebrows frame the face and are more important than most women realize. Very messy, thick eyebrow can make the eyes appear smaller. Therefore, go to an eyebrow threading salon to get your eyebrows cleaned up.

SMALL NOSE

The smaller a nose is, the better. A large nose is the one facial feature that sticks out and the larger it is the more distracting it is to others. The less noticeable it is, the more noticeable other facial features are, such as the eyes. Simply by reducing the size or shape of the nose a person can look much more attractive.

The only permanent method of reducing the size of the nose is a nose job (rhinoplasty). You can also try a non-surgical nose job if the main problem is a bump on the top of the nose.

IMMACULATE SKIN

People that have skin with ugly flaws are automatically labeled less attractive. Both men and women can use makeup to cover up obvious flaws. According to Makeup Alley Product Reviews (www.makeupalley.com) Estee Lauder Double Wear is ranked one of the best foundations and Make Up For Ever Full Cover Concealer and MAC Pro Longwear concealer are ranked the best concealers.

To achieve immaculate skin you must thoroughly cleanse and care for your skin. The three basic steps to good skin care are: cleanse, treat, and moisturize.

According to Makeup Alley Product Reviews (www.makeupalley.com), the highest rated and most reviewed skin care tool is Clarisonic Pro Skincare Brush. The highest rated and most reviewed facial cleansers are Ponds Deep Cleanser Cold Cream, Purpose Gentle Cleansing Wash, MAC Cleanse Off Oil, Bioderma Sensibio H2O, and Olay Sensitive Skin Foaming Face Wash.

The highest rated and most reviewed skin treatments are Paula's Choice Skin Perfecting 2% BHA Lotion Exfoliant, Clean & Clear Persagel 10, Acne.org Treatment, Philosophy Resurface Kit, Alpha Hydrox AHA Souffle 12 percent Glycolic AHA, Neutrogena Oil-Free Acne Stress Control 3-in-1 Hydrating Acne Treatment, and Estee Lauder Advanced Night Repair Serum,

The highest rated and most reviewed moisturizers are Cetaphil Moisturizing Cream, Desert Essence Jojoba Oil, Weleda Skin Food, Clinique Dramatically Different Moisturizing Gel, CeraVe Moisturizing Lotion, Olay Complete with SPF 15 Lotion, Garnier Moisture Rescue Refreshing Gel-Cream, MAC Strobe Cream, Eucerin Q10 Anti-Wrinkle Sensitive Skin Crème, Avene Skin Recovery Cream, and Alpha Hydrox 10% Enhanced Cream.

In adolescence, oily skin and acne are the most common skin flaws. According to Treato (www.treato.com), over 1,000,000 patients found Differin to be the most effective topical treatment for acne. Minocycline and Retin A came in second. Over 100,000 patients ranked Clearasil the best treatment for oily skin.

In adults, dry skin and wrinkles are the most common skin flaws. According to Treato (www.treato.com), over 200,000 patients found Aquaphor the best treatment for dry skin. Over 100,000 patients ranked Retin A the best treatment for wrinkles, followed by Restylane.

To treat serious skin imperfections you will need to go to an experienced cosmetic dermatologist. The CO_2 laser will eliminate discoloration, scars, warts, enlarged pores, freckles, age spots, fines lines, and wrinkles. A photofacial will remove broken capillaries, sun damage, enlarged pores, freckles, age spots, redness, rosacea, fine lines, and wrinkles. Fraxel removes wrinkles, sun damage, age spots, acne scarring, and skin discoloration.

An experienced cosmetic dermatologist can help eliminate many skin flaws, but a naturopath or holistic physician can treat major skin flaws that a dermatologist is unable to treat such as severe acne, eczema, psoriasis, or rosacea.

IMPECCABLE HAIR

One of the first things people notice and remember about you is your hair color, hair length, hair style, and how healthy your hair looks. Tradition plays a huge role in how hair should look in men and in women.

A poll of over 600 voters on Mister Poll (http://www.misterpoll.com/polls/247007/results) found that the three most attractive hair colors in women are brunette, red, and blonde. Light blonde, dirty blonde, dark red, dark brunette, and black are the most preferred hair shades on a woman (http://www.misterpoll.com/polls/146045/results).

There is a common debate about whether blondes or brunette women are hotter. A poll of over 9000 voters on Mister Poll (http://www.misterpoll.com/polls/93838/results) found that men ranked blonde and brunette hair about the same.

Voters on Mister Poll (http://www.misterpoll.com/polls/96385/results) ranked straight, shoulder length hair or longer as the most attractive on women.

The traditional look for men is dark-colored hair. In numerous surveys and polls, a vast amount of women prefers men with dark-colored hair. Voters on Mister Poll (http://www.misterpoll.com/polls/247007/results) rated brown the most attractive hair color on a man. The second most attractive color on a man is black.

Voters on Mister Poll (http://www.misterpoll.com/polls/421475/results) rated short hair the most attractive on men. Crewcut and short flat hair (less than one inch) were most preferred (http://www.misterpoll.com/polls/141820/results).

According to Makeup Alley Product Reviews (www.makeupalley.com), the highest rated and most reviewed hair coloring products are Garnier Nutrisse Permanent Creme Hair Color, Revlon Colorsilk, Clairol Natural Instincts Hair Color, and L'Oreal Excellence Crème.

To achieve shiny and healthy looking hair you must use the absolute best shampoo and conditioner available on the market. According to Makeup Alley Product Reviews (www.makeupalley.com), the highest rated and most reviewed shampoo is Redken All Soft Shampoo. Neutrogena Anti-Residue Shampoo and Suave Daily Clarifying Shampoo are also highly rated. The highest rated and most reviewed conditioner are Redken All Soft Conditioner, Neutrogena Triple Moisture Deep Recovery Hair Mask, and Matrix Biolage Conditioning Balm.

The highest rated and most reviewed hair styling products according to Makeup Alley Product Reviews (www.makeupalley.com) are Frederic Fekkai Glossing Cream with Olive Oil and Paul Mitchell Super Skinny Serum.

FIT BODY

For women, thin is in. For men, a medium muscular tanned build is considered attractive. Being extremely overweight and extremely underweight in both men and women is considered very unattractive.

Voters on Mister Poll (http://www.misterpoll.com/polls/136452/results) rated a tanned, medium built body the most attractive on men. Besides the face, muscular abs are ranked the most important body part in a man.

Voters on Mister Poll (http://www.misterpoll.com/polls/434746/results) rated a slim body the most attractive for women. Anorexic and obese body types are considered the least attractive.

According to Treato (www.treato.com), over 5,000,000 patients rated Topamax the best medication for losing weight, followed by Metformin and Phentermine.

According to Real Self (www.realself.com/reviews), the best surgery methods to reduce overeating are gastric bypass, sleeve gastrectomy, and lap band. The best method to target specific areas of fat on the body is tumescent liposuction, lipotherme, SmartLipo, SlimLipo, Liposonix, CoolSculpting, and Body Jet Liposuction.

For those that are extremely skinny, according to Treato (www.treato.com), over 1,000,000 patients rated Megace the best treatment for helping one to gain weight.

TURN-OFFS

The Urban Dictionary (www.urbandictionary.com) defines a turn-off as something that disgusts people. Disgusting features include yellow or crooked teeth, body order, nasal hair, bad breath, facial hair, messy hair, dirty nails.

There are a few big turn-offs for both men and women that must be addressed if one is to attain popularity and attract the opposite sex.

Tattoos on women are the biggest turn off for men. Beards are what women are least attracted to, with a third of those questioned voting hairy faces the most disgusting feature. Bad breath came second on the lists of both men and women. Excessive piercings are rated as unattractive in both men and women (Source: http://www.dailymail.co.uk/femail/article-2173101/Tattoos-bad-breath-beards-bitten-nails-What-men-women-biggest-turn-offs-opposite-sex.html).

The most obvious ways to make sure you don't turn off others is to shower twice a day, use breath fresheners and deodorant religiously, remove excess hair, whiten and straighten teeth, wash hair every day, get manicures once a week, and don't get any tattoos or body and facial piercings.

For excessive sweating and odor, miraDry is a non-invasive treatment that reduces excessive sweating permanently. It uses microwave energy to eliminate underarm sweat glands.

According to Makeup Alley Product Reviews (www.makeupalley.com), the highest rated and most reviewed body cleansing products are St. Ives Oatmeal and Shea Butter Body Wash, Dove Beauty Bar, Philosophy Cinnamon Buns 3-in-1, and The Body Shop Satsuma Shower Gel.

According to Makeup Alley Product Reviews (www.makeupalley.com), the highest rated and most reviewed teeth whitening system is Plus White 5 Minute Speed Whitening Gel.

According to Real Self (www.realself.com/reviews), the best method to straighten teeth is Invisalign (www.invisalign.com).

According to Makeup Alley Product Reviews (www.makeupalley.com), the highest rated and most reviewed breath fresheners are Aveda Peppymint Breath Refresher and Burt's Bees Peppermint Breath Drops.

Electrolysis is a permanent hair removal method that uses an electrical current. Intense Pulsed Light (IPL) and laser hair removal keep unwanted hairs away for a long time but are not permanent. Laser hair removal uses a laser while IPL uses a light-based device. You can buy at-home devices for hair removal. The Tria laser is a laser home device, and Silk'n SensEpil is an IPL home device.

According to Makeup Alley Product Reviews (www.makeupalley.com), the highest rated and most reviewed deodorants are Crystal Body Deodorant Stick, Kiehls Superbly Efficient Anti-Perspirant and Deodorant Cream, Donna Karan Cashmere Mist Deodorant, Lady Mitchum Dry Roll-On Antiperspirant And Deodorant, Thai

Deodorant Crystal, and Vichy Deodorant-Antiperspirant 48 Hours.

Wearing delicious smelling fragrances are a huge turn on and both men and women should wear a high rated fragrance. According to Makeup Alley Product Reviews (www.makeupalley.com), the highest rated and most reviewed men's fragrances are Giorgio Armani Acqua Di Gio, Givenchy Pi, Victoria's Secret Very Sexy For Him, Liz Claiborne Curve for Men, Burberry Touch for Men, Davidoff Cool Water For Men, Chanel Platinum Egoiste, Giorgio Armani Black Code, and Issey Miyake L'eau D'issey Pour Homme.

The highest rated and most reviewed women's fragrances are Chanel Coco Mademoiselle, Burberry Brit, Stella McCartney Stella, Victoria's Secret Dream Angels Heavenly, Juicy Couture Viva La Juicy, Chanel Allure, and Chanel Coco.

CHAPTER TWO

FASHION SENSE

Fashion sense relates to the most popular look of the moment. "Fashion is made to become unfashionable," said French fashion designer Coco Chanel. Therefore, fashion sense implies wearing the latest fashion trends in clothing, shoes, and accessories. Fashion trends only last a season.

Men can keep with up with fashion trends by flipping through *GQ, Esquire, Details, Men's Vogue,* and *Complex* magazine.

Women can keep up with fashion trends by flipping through *Vogue, Elle, Cosmopolitan, InStyle,* and *Harper's Bazaar* magazine.

Men and women that wear designer brands tend to achieve a higher status in social groups. Wearing designer brands conveys the message that you have money and good taste, two factors that many people value and respect.

Top designer brands include the following: Valentino, Gucci, Prada, Versace, Louis Vuitton, Chanel, Diane Von Furstenberg, Marc Jacobs, Prabal Gurung, Stella Mccartney, Calvin Klein, Armani, Alexander McQueen, Dolce & Gabbana, Manolo Blahnik, Christian Dior, Yves Saint

Laurent, Ralph Lauren, Jimmy Choo, Burberry, Christian Louboutin, and Hermés.

CLOTHING AND SHOES

The starting point to dressing fashionably is to note what colors and styles of clothing and shoes are in for the season. Then you need to purchase these colors and styles for the season. Ideally, you would purchase fashionable items from top designer brands stores or online (Women: www.net-a-porter.com Men: www.mrporter.com). If you are on a budget you can purchase fashionable items from H&M and American Apparel.

Everyone should have fundamental clothing items that go with everything. You can wear fashionable clothing with simple, fundamental clothing and shoes. For example, you can wear a fashionable, designer top, with simple black pants. You can wear very bright-colored shoes with a simple all-black outfit. Fundamental, basic clothing items are very simple, with no patterns, and are typically black and sometimes white or neutral-colored. Fundamental clothing items can be purchased at H&M and American Apparel.

Fundamental, basic clothing items for men include neutral-colored trench coat, black blazer, black turtleneck sweater, black cardigan sweater, black pants, black shorts, black sleeveless tank top, and black classic oxford shoes.

Fundamental, basic clothing items for women include neutral-colored trench coat, black blazer, black turtleneck sweater, black cardigan sweater, black sheath dress, black shell top, black V-neck halter top, black slim-leg pants, black pencil skirt, black shirts, and black 4-inch high-heel classic pumps.

The most important rule of fashion sense is to never wear the same outfit two days in a row. You must always wear a new outfit every day.

ACCESSORIES

Designer accessories are even more important than designer clothing and are a better investment because they can typically be worn for longer than one season.

Designer accessories such as sunglasses, hats, watches, bags, and scarves, can be worn with any outfit and for many seasons.

A very valuable accessory for both men and women to wear are designer sunglasses. Ideally, invest in designer brand sunglasses that look good on your face and are classic in style, rather than on ones that are trendy and may no longer be fashionable in a season or two.

A very valuable accessory for a man to wear is a luxury designer watch; the more expensive the better. Besides clothing, many people judge a man by the watch that he wears. If you are on a budget it is better not to wear a watch at all, than to wear a cheap or knock-off watch. Top luxury designer watches include Rolex, Patek Philippe, Breguet, Breitling, Cartier, Jaeger-LeCoultre, Audemars Piquet, Blancpain, IWC, and Hublot.

A valuable accessory for a woman to have is a designer handbag. Women judge other women on the handbag that they carry. The more expensive the handbag, the better. Exclusive hard-to-get "it" handbags (waiting list required) are the ultimate women's accessory and will get serious attention from women. Top designer handbags include Hermés, Chanel, Prada, Louis Vuitton, Michael Kors, Gucci, Christian Dior, Alexander McQueen, Mulberry, Yves Saint Laurent, Balenciaga, Miu, and Chloe.

Accessories such as classic style hats and scarves can be worn on occasion if it contributes to and matches an outfit. For men, the fedora is the classic hat and for women, the wide-brimmed sun hat is classic. For both men and women, classic scarves are available from Burberry and Louis Vuitton.

Men should not wear jewelry or wear very minimal jewelry since the wearing of jewelry is portrayed as feminine. Simple, silver jewelry is acceptable for men.

Women can wear jewelry such as necklaces, bracelets, and earrings to enhance any outfit. The more expensive the jewelry, the better. Tiffany & Co is a top jewelry designer brand.

CHAPTER THREE

PERSONALITY

Fashion sense relates to the most popular look of the moment. "Fashion is made to become unfashionable," said French fashion designer Coco Chanel. Therefore, fashion sense implies wearing the latest fashion trends in clothing, shoes, and accessories. Fashion trends only last a season.

Behavior, known as your personality, determines your status of popularity. A person's behavior is ruled by their psychological health, hormonal levels, and self-confidence.

Although there are many personality traits, there are only three personality traits that are important in the popularity game: social attitude, femininity/masculinity, and self-confidence. People can alter their personality with medications, natural supplements, and therapies to change how others perceive them and gain higher popularity status.

SOCIAL ATTITUDE

Your social attitude towards people is the way you think and behave when you are dealing with them. When a person has a well-developed, positive social attitude, they command respect. The stronger your social attitude, the stronger will be your impact in social settings and the higher your popularity status.

To develop a positive social attitude, you must know yourself and develop a strong sense of who you are. You must love who you are as a person, and know what you like and dislike and be able to express your opinions in a vivid way. The most common way to get to know oneself is through taking various personality tests. You can obtain personality tests from books or online. Other methods of getting to know oneself are by visiting an astrologist, numerologist, or palmist.

Personality disorders can greatly affect how you interact with others and determine how others treat you. There are different types of personality disorders: Paranoid, Schizoid, Schizotypal, Antisocial, Borderline, Histrionic, Narcissistic, Avoidant, Dependent, and Obsessive-Compulsive. There are symptoms for each type of personality disorder (http://www.mayoclinic.com/health/personality-disorders/DS00562/DSECTION=symptoms).

An evaluation by a psychiatrist, a medical intuitive scan, aura imagery, quantum biofeedback, and electrodermal screening will help diagnose personality disorders.

The most common personality disorders that result in low social hierarchy are social anxiety disorder and avoidant personality disorder.

People with social anxiety disorder feel quite anxious or fearful in social situations. They are very concerned that they will do something embarrassing and that others will think badly of them.

Social anxiety disorder can be treated with prescription drugs and natural supplements such as vitamins or herbs.

passion flower, valerian root, winter cherry, and 5-HTP are known to treat social anxiety disorder. There are several types of medications used to treat social anxiety disorder. Selective serotonin reuptake inhibitors (SSRIs) are often the first type of medication tried for persistent symptoms of social anxiety. SSRIs your doctor may prescribe include: Paroxetine (Paxil), Sertraline (Zoloft), Fluoxetine (Prozac) and Fluvoxamine (Luvox).

Avoidant personality disorder is characterized by social inhibition, extreme sensitivity to negative evaluation, avoidance of social interaction, and severe low self-esteem. Some medications that have been found to be successful for the treatment of avoidant personality disorder are Monoamine Oxidase Inhibitors like Parnate, Marplan, and Nardil. These drugs help the individual cope with avoidant personality disorder by improving their confidence level.

Besides drugs and natural supplements, social anxiety disorder, avoidant personality disorder, and other personality disorders can also be treated with different forms of psychotherapy.

Bioenergetic analysis and therapy is a form of psychotherapy shown to reduce symptoms of social insecurity, depression, anxiety, anger, and hostility.

Emotional freedom techniques (EFT) can effectively treat personality disorders. It works to immediately reduce phobia-related anxiety.

Advanced integrative therapy (AIT) is a type of energy psychotherapy that treats a wide range of personality disorders.

Cognitive behavior therapy (CBT) changes thinking patterns. Changing thinking patterns changes emotions and behavior. CBT can treat depression, anxiety, panic disorder, social phobia, and post-traumatic stress disorder (PTSD).

Psychoanalysis and psychodynamic therapy are both similar forms of a type of psychotherapy. These types of psychotherapy treat various personality disorders.

The brain dramatically influences social behavior, thoughts, and feelings. A SPECT scan will help determine causes of personality disorders. SPECT scans, performed by certain physiatrists, can determine the improper functioning of different parts of the brain and neurotransmitter imbalances.

For those that don't have a personality disorder and would simply like to develop a positive social attitude, there are therapies that can do that. The Silva Method, Mettā meditation, Gestalt therapy, DNA Theta Healing, Wholistic hybrid of EMDR and EFT (WHEE), and Hypnosis may increase positive social behaviors and attitudes and remove negative social personality traits.

FEMININITY/MASCULINITY

Femininity is a set of attributes, behaviors, and roles associated with females. Traits traditionally associated with femininity include being emotional, caring, sweet, gentle, compassionate, and sensitive.

Masculinity is a set of qualities, characteristics or roles considered typical of men. Traits traditionally associated with masculinity include non-emotional, aggressive, tough, competitive, strong, and independent.

If you aren't naturally acting like your gender, you may consider hormone testing to determine if you are lacking essential hormones that determine your behavior. You can get hormone tests online or through a doctor or naturopath. You can get blood, saliva, or urine hormone testing.

You can consider taking prescription drugs or natural supplements if you are lacking essential hormones. An increase in female hormone (estrogen) will promote feminine behavior while an increase in male hormone (testosterone) will promote masculine behavior.

Two herbs that are known to naturally increase male hormone in the body are tribulus terrestris and eurycoma longifolia jack. Prescription medication such as AndroGel (topical testosterone gel) or Testosterone Undecanoate can be prescribed by a doctor.

Herbs known to naturally increase female hormone in the body are pueraria mirifica and licorice root. Prescription medication such as Oestrogel (topical estradiol gel) or Estradiol Valerate can be prescribed by a doctor.

SELF-CONFIDENCE

Self-confidence means having confidence in yourself, your abilities, and your social interactions. You need to like yourself before others can like you. We show people how to treat us by the way we treat ourselves.

You can increase your self-confidence by using positive affirmations, visualization, flower essences, energy supplements, and prescription medications.

Autosuggestion is a psychological technique, commonly called positive affirmations. Positive affirmations repeated every day such as, "I am self-confident," or "I am confident around people," can transform the way you behave. You can actually train yourself to be confident. A repeated thought, or feeling, can become reality over time, although only to the extent that the idea is within the realm of possibility (Source: *Self-Mastery Through Conscious Autosuggestion* by Émile Coué).

Studies have shown that the brain cannot distinguish from a real or an imaginary picture. The same chemicals release and the same electrical activity displays in the brain whether we are visualizing something or actually doing it. (Source: *Maximum Influence: The 12 Universal Laws of Power Persuasion* by Mortensen, Kurt W. and Robert G. Allen).

In 2007, Harvard Medical School conducted a study with volunteers who were asked to learn and practice a piano exercise. A neuroscientist instructed half of the volunteers to practice playing, two hours a day for five days. The other half were instructed to merely think about practicing the piano, holding their hands still while playing the music in their heads. At the end of the five days, both groups underwent a transcranial-magnetic-stimulation test. The test results showed that the same region of the brain had expanded in the volunteers who merely thought about playing. This study shows that the brain doesn't distinguish between a real or imagined exercise.

Close your eyes for half an hour to an hour every day and visualize that you are behaving confidently in social settings.

Flower essences are infusions of herbs in water. Flower essences are used to help treat emotional, mental, and spiritual imbalances. Limitations and disharmonies begin to change (Source: http://www.essencesonline.com/FESQuints.htm#Availability.

Cosmos flower essence helps with integration of ideas and speech; coherent thinking; mercurial expression and helps eliminate unfocused, disorganized communication; and overexcited speech.

Trumpet Vine flower essence helps with articulate and colorful verbal expression; active, dynamic projection of oneself in social situations and eliminates lack of vitality in expression; inability to be assertive or to speak clearly, and speech impediments.

Violet flower essence helps eliminate profound shyness, reserve, aloof, and fear of being submerged in groups.

Self-confident, popular people have higher energy levels than less popular people. Energy supplements can increase a person's self-confidence with people. Research shows that the combination of caffeine, taurine, and glucuronolactone, found in energy drinks, increases social extrovertedness. (Source: http://www.ncbi.nlm.nih.gov/pubmed/11140366). Drink energy drinks or take natural energy supplements before socializing.

Propranolol or other beta-blockers help some people increase self-confidence interaction with people and reduce panic during public-speaking. Research shows that propranolol helps promote more social and adaptive behaviors (Source: http://www.ncbi.nlm.nih.gov/pubmed/3654495). According to Treato (www.treato.com), patients reported that Propranolol helped them when used for panic (33% higher than the average of other panic treatments).

CHAPTER FOUR

SOCIAL SKILLS

Social skills relate to social communication and behavior. Research shows that those that are unpopular do not have proper social skills. (Source: *Social Skills Assessment and Training with Children* by Don P. Sugai, Randy P. Wood, Alan E. Kazdin and Larry Michelson) Those with better social skills tend to have higher social status and social acceptance. (Source: Putallaz, M. (1983). Predicting Children's Sociometric Status from Their Behavior. *Child Development*, 54(6), 1417-1426).

Popularity results from three major social skills: assertion skills, leadership skills, and polarity. All three social skills must incorporate a level of kindness and fairness. Bo Bennett once said, "True popularity comes from acts of kindness rather than acts of stupidity."

ASSERTION SKILLS

Assertiveness is a social skill in which you demonstrate poise and are able to defend yourself and your rights when others try and put you down while still respecting others. It can sometimes mean dealing with others in a fairly aggressive manner if they disrespect you.

Most unpopular people are passive or overly aggressive. Passive people don't defend themselves, and let others abuse or manipulate them through fear. Aggressiveness, while definitely appropriate in some instances, isn't a very productive communication or behavior style in most cases. In fact, being overly aggressive can often backfire by creating resentment and aggression from those you are acting aggressively toward.

Instead of being passive or aggressive, the best approach lies somewhere between the two. The best method for communication and behavior is assertiveness.

According to Randy Paterson, Ph.D., a clinical psychologist and author of The Assertiveness Workbook: How to Express Your Ideas and Stand Up for Yourself at Work and in Relationships, assertiveness means you're able to articulate your wants and needs to the other people.

Assertiveness is a skill that takes practice (Source: http://www.ncbi.nlm.nih.gov/pmc/articles/PMC1311169/). Assertion skills are best learned through taking an assertion skills course available through your local personal development center.

A study found that reboxetine, a drug of the norepinephrine reuptake inhibitor class, enhances assertive social behavior. In the study, is was observed that reboxetine makes healthy volunteers more self-confident and assertive (Source: http://www.ncbi.nlm.nih.gov/pubmed/16944408).

LEADERSHIP SKILLS

Being a leader requires a well-developed personality. It requires being able to get and then maintain the respect of many followers through powerful communication, strength, dominance, charisma, extraversion, and influence. There is evidence to show that leadership develops through hard work and careful observation (Forsyth, D. R. (2009). *Group dynamics (5th ed.)*. Pacific Grove, CA: Brooks/Cole). Thus, effective leadership can be learned.

Leadership is mostly about behavior. You can assume the role of a leader among a group of people and maintain that leadership through your behavior.

Leadership skills can best be observed and learned through wolves. The alpha male wolf is the leader of a pack of wolves. He is highly respected and the toughest among the group of wolves. He controls the activities of the group of wolves he leads. He gains and maintains his position of leadership of the pack through dominant behavior and, if necessary, through an aggressive assertion (a fight). The alpha female is the leader of the pack alongside the male. The alpha male and female communicate their dominance through eye contact and aggressive assertion. Read books and study videos of the behavior of the alpha wolves.

Those with no knowledge of leadership skills can learn through leadership skills courses and seminars. Without proper leadership training, it can take many painful years of trial and error to learn the techniques needed to lead a group effectively. An extrovert course can also be very helpful for those who need to overcome shyness and socialization problems. An extrovert drug such as Paxil may be considered if the problem persists.

POLARITY

Being too nice or polite can actually push people away as can being too mean and too cruel. Instead, be polar and hard to figure out. Polarity gives one popularity.

Polarity is defined as being in opposite extremes. It means to be a contradiction. Robert Greene, the author of *The Art of Seduction*, says, "Send mixed signals: both tough and tender, both spiritual and earthy, both innocent and cunning. A mix of qualities suggests depth, which fascinates even as it confuses. An elusive, enigmatic aura will make people want to know more, drawing them into your circle."

Leaders of a group have a combination of meanness and kindness. Be very kind and charming at times, and assertive at other times. Study the movies *Mean Girls* and *The New Guy*, and you will notice the most popular people are those that have mastered the skill of polarity. Study the book The Art of Seduction to master the skills of polarity.

A perfect balance of kindness and assertiveness will lead to popularity. Typically, you should be kind 50% of the time and assertive 50% of the time.

Being kind and charming is about making others feel good through pleasant speech such as compliments or behavior such as smiling. Brian Tracy, a personal and professional development expert, said, "Charm is the ability to create extraordinary rapport that makes others feel exceptional." American writer Maya Angelou said, "I've learned that people will forget what you said, people will forget what you did, but people will never forget how you made them feel."

Compliments make a person feel good. Abraham Lincoln, the sixteenth president of the United States, said, "Everybody likes a compliment." Be very specific with your compliments and give them out to the right people.

Smiling can increase or decrease an individual's attractiveness and charm. A study has found that smiling women are considered more attractive, while men are considered less attractive when they smile (Jessica L. Tracy, Alec T. Beall. Happy guys finish last: The impact of emotion expressions on sexual attraction. *Emotion*, 11(6), 1379-1387). The researchers suggest that smiling men were judged to be more feminine and less dominant and therefore less attractive. In all cases, men rated smiling women highest. Proud women were rated lower. Women rated the proud men highest. They rated smiling men lower (http://www.cbc.ca/news/technology/smiling-men-less-attractive-to-women-study-1.1066058).

.

CHAPTER FIVE

STATUS SYMBOLS

A status symbol is a visible, outward denotation of one's social position. All popular people have some sort of status symbols. People judge an individual based on their status symbols. Many luxury goods are often considered status symbols. Status symbols may change in value or meaning over time. Relationships can also be considered status symbols.

WEALTH

Being wealthy and showing it through material possessions will automatically give you a higher social position. Material possessions typically perceived as status symbols may include a mansion or penthouse, fashionable clothes, expensive jewelry, expensive electronics, fancy cell phones, or a luxury vehicle. The possession of a privately owned aircraft and luxury yachts will further increase social status.

Having good taste is essential if you are wealthy. You want to own material possession that people admire. Websites such as www.trendhunter.com and www.robbreport.com highlight the latest luxury products and trends.

Being perceived as wealthy is very difficult if you aren't actually wealthy or if you have a mediocre household income. Creating wealth takes study, hard-work, and dedication, but can be done at any age, as young as twelve and even as old as retirement age. Study books such as *Think and Grow Rich*, *Millionaire Fastlane*, *The $100 Startup*, *Laptop Millionaire*, and *The 4-Hour Workweek*, among many other great business books.

Massive wealth is created through starting a business either online or in your local area, selling a service or a product, or investing in real estate or other assets that appreciate in value.

CLASS

Classy people dress and behave in a somewhat conservative manner. "Some people think luxury is the opposite of poverty. It is not. It is the opposite of vulgarity," said Coco Chanel. People of very high social class and women of royalty dress and behave conservatively. Duchess Kate Middleton and Prince William are a great example of dressing and acting conservatively to convey class.

Dressing in a classy manner means dressing in conservative, high-quality clothing. Although designer brand clothing is typically considered classy, high-quality clothing can also convey class. High-quality clothing is made from natural fibers such as silk, wool, cotton, cashmere, and linen among others. Observe how wealthy individuals and royalty dress and mimic their style.

Acting conservatively means behaving in a modest, polite, friendly manner. Being conservative does not mean being quiet or shy. It means acting dignified and demanding respect from others while still being very social and talkative.

RELATIONSHIPS

Being in a relationship with a popular and/or very attractive person will automatically give you a higher social position. Being friends with very popular or famous individuals will also result in popularity.

In high school, for a woman to be in a relationship with a very attractive and very popular man will automatically increase her social status. In adulthood, marriage to a man with impressive status symbols will fortify her social status. To attract good-looking men or wealthy men with status symbols a woman must make herself as visually attractive as possible.

For a man to be in a relationship with a very attractive woman will lift his social status as well as earn him respect and admiration from his peers. In some social circles, a man will be admired and respected by his peers for dating numerous attractive women. For a man to be in a relationship with an unattractive woman may actually lower his social status. In adulthood, a man's marriage to a "trophy wife" will fortify his social status. A "trophy wife" is a woman of exceptional beauty, with looks comparable to those of a supermodel.

For a man to acquire an attractive woman, he needs to demonstrate alpha male characteristics. In different stages of life, women are attracted to different types of men. In general, women in high school and younger are particularly attracted to men with good looks and good athlete ability. Women out of high school tend to value men with status symbols and focus slightly less on good looks and athletic ability. This is why it is fairly common to see exceptionally beautiful women with less attractive men as long as they possess impressive status symbols.

RESOURCES

Physical Beauty

Real Self (www.realself.com/reviews)

Makeup Alley (www.makeupalley.com)

Sephora (www.sephora.com)

Skin Store (www.skinstore.com)

Derm Store (www.dermstore.com)

Fashion Sense

Women's Fashion (www.net-a-porter.com)

Men's Fashion (www.mrporter.com)

H&M (www.hm.com)

Topshop (www.topshop.com)

Warehouse (www.warehouse.co.uk)

Oasis (www.oasis-stores.com)

Personality

Prescription Drug Reviews (www.treato.com)

Flower Essences (www.essencesonline.com)

Natural Supplements (www.iherb.com)

Social Skills

Extrovert Course (www.extrovertme.com)

Assertion (www.speakupforyourself.com/freeclass.htm)

Status Symbols

Trend Hunter (www.trendhunter.com)

Robb Report (www.robbreport.com)

Beautiful People Dating (www.beautifulpeople.com)

Darwin Dating (www.darwindating.com)

Good Looking Dating (www.goodlookingdating.com)

.